Daily Prayer Book for Girls

CONVERSATIONS WITH GOD

FaithLabs

THIS BOOK BELONGS TO:

. . . .

. . . .

. . . .

. . . .

Daily Prayer Book *for* Girls

CONVERSATIONS WITH GOD

Don't Forget Your Free Bonus Downloads!

As our way of saying thank you, we've included in every purchase bonus gift downloads. If you've enjoyed reading this book, please consider leaving a review.

Or Scan Your Phone to open QR code

Conversations with God

Prayer Books for Girls :
Daily Prayer Book for Girls

Contents

INTRODUCTION

"But thou, when thou prayest, enter into thy closet, and when thou hast shut thy door, pray to thy Father which is in secret; and thy Father which seeth in secret shall reward thee openly."

- Matthew 6:6

Do you desire to strengthen your spirituality? Do you wish to do miracles as you go? Is there hope for a remake? In order to spread the Good News to unreached areas and prepare people for the Second Coming of Jesus Christ? All these things come naturally to us because we are disciples of Jesus. Seeing God's kingdom established on earth as it is in heaven is something we long for deeply and leaves us wanting more. However, the price of desire is high. Not without some effort on our part, unfortunately.

Having a close relationship with God is an effort we need to make.

Our first focus should be our close relationship. We need to be in a close connection with God if we're going to perform God's job God's way. This implies that we seek to know God's will through reading His Word, conversing with Him, and listening for His voice. This is the essence of praying. Praying is just talking to God. We commune with Him via prayer, song, Scripture reading, and quiet reflection. A close relationship is vital because it provides strength and encouragement, particularly during trying times in ministry or in life. Jesus forewarned us of trouble; He alone can calm us through it.

So, what does it mean to persist steadfastly? How can we, as Christians, persevere in this chaotic and fallen world? Committing to praying regularly might be useful in this regard. First on Jesus's list of suggestions for what to ask for in prayer was "give us this day our daily bread." Thus, we shall need daily replenishment of our stock. If we don't pray daily, we'll have to make do with yesterday's bread, which may have become hard and stale by now. The Christian faith is meant to be a dynamic, everyday experience with the living God. No matter how dry or terrible the season is, we may push each day to grow in our relationship with God. Prayer helps us discover the living water and daily food that sustain us through the dry periods until spring.

Because our God is wonderful, He has made us need to pray to Him daily. By communicating with God, prayer brings us closer to the one who gives us meaning and happiness. Our needs will be met when we communicate with the One who has everything. Even if prayer seems obscure, don't underestimate its significance. You'll need it if you want to live a life of doing God's will. A few things will improve your relationship with God, like making time daily to pray, ideally for an hour or more. Make a decision and stick to it even if it's challenging.

The following sections include a variety of prayers that may be said on a daily basis and serve as a reminder to keep our commitment to prayer.

PART 1

Prayers for Everyday

Praise in the Morning Prayer

*

"By Him, therefore, let us offer the sacrifice of praise to God continually, that is, the fruit of our lips giving thanks to his name. But to do good and to communicate, forget not: for with such sacrifices, God is well pleased."

Hebrews 13:15-16

Prayer

Father, I promise I will never stop singing your praises. You are deserving of the highest praise and the highest honor. I will never miss an opportunity to spread the good news of your goodness to those I cross paths with. You are fantastic, lovely, and wonderful! In Jesus'name, amen.

*

Reflection

God deserves all praise for all he has done for us. In what ways do you glorify God in your daily life? How can you persuade others to believe in God?

Prayer of Thanks to God

"Sing unto the Lord with thanksgiving; sing praise upon the harp unto our God."

Psalms 147:7

Prayer

Father, my heart sings happy because you woke me up this morning and kept me warm all night. I'm thankful for all the good things that have happened to me and what you've done for me. You are compassionate and caring, and you are concerned about me. I will talk about your good deeds all day long. Thank you for always being there. In Jesus' name, amen.

Reflection

Each day is a gift from God. What is the most recent blessing God has bestowed upon you? How have you shown gratitude to God for this blessing?

Prayer of Hope

Moreover whom he did predestinate, whom he also called: and whom he called, whom he also justified: and whom he justified, whom he also glorified. What shall we then say to these things? If God is for us, who can be against us?

Romans 8:30-31

Prayer

Father God, I know you are good and can do miracles. Even though I'm having a hard time and my heart is heavy, I still want to bless you. I know that no matter what happens, you are still good and can make the best of any situation that comes your way. I thank you ahead of time for your answer and your help. In Jesus'name, amen.

Reflection

We all have difficult times and meet obstacles. What do you do when confronted with obstacles? How do you conquer the difficulties in your life?

Prayer of Divine Favor

*

Let the words of my mouth, and the meditation of my heart, be acceptable in thy sight, O Lord, my strength, and my redeemer.

Psalms 19:14

Prayer

May the words I speak today, Father God, please the Lord of my strength. The one and only maker! You have rescued me from the depths of my sin, O Lord. I pray that the way I live will please you. Please help me lay out a productive day. I ask that the people I interact with have their hearts warmed by you. In the name of Jesus, amen.

*

Reflection

God desired for us to live a moral life. How do you spend your daily life in accordance with God's will? How do you demonstrate compassion to strangers?

Prayer for Productivity

*

"And whatsoever ye do, do it heartily, as to the Lord, and not unto men."

Colossians 3:23

Prayer

Lord, I pray that the things I create today will honor you. Please remind me that all I do is for your honor and praise. Enlighten me that my best work is a means through which you may be praised. I need your assistance in keeping my mind on the work at hand. In the name of Jesus, amen.

*

Reflection

Daily, we should glorify God through the simplest actions. How can one honor God while at home? In what ways might your hobbies be used to glorify God?

Prayer for Safety

For he shall give his angels charge over thee, to keep thee in all thy ways.

Psalms 91:11

Prayer

Father, Please know how much I appreciate the sanctuary and security you've provided me. Please accept my gratitude for keeping my family and myself safe as we go about our day. Please, God, watch over my loved ones and make sure they're always safe. To the extent possible, please shield us from harm. In the name of Jesus, amen.

*

Reflection

God is ever there to guide and protect us. How do you know that God always protects you? From what danger would you desire your family to be protected?

Prayer for Confidence

But I will sing of thy power; yea, I will sing aloud of thy mercy in the morning: for thou hast been my defense and refuge in the day of my trouble.

Psalms 59:16

Prayer

My trust, Heavenly Father, is in you alone. I don't brag about how capable I am; rather, I brag about how capable we are when we work together via you. I go forth into today certain that you are with me and that your almighty hand will lead me in the right direction. Your care for me and your companionship are both wonderful gifts. I pray this in the name of Jesus. amen.

❋

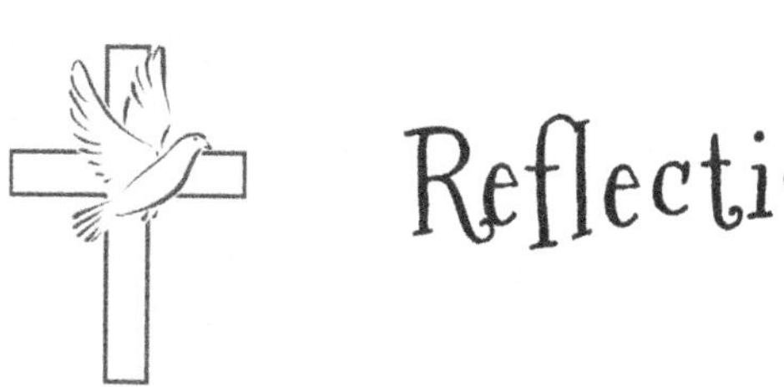

Reflection

God will always be at our side no matter what we do. How do you perceive God to be for you? What are the benefits of maintaining a close connection with God?

Prayer for Boldness

*

For God hath not given us the spirit of fear; but of power, love, and a sound mind.

2 Timothy 1:7

Prayer

I ask, Father, that you bless me with the kind of godly confidence that comes from knowing you as I go into today. Inspire me to represent you as I speak the truth in love and act on my God-given talents. Your holiness covers me like a robe. In the name of Jesus, amen.

*

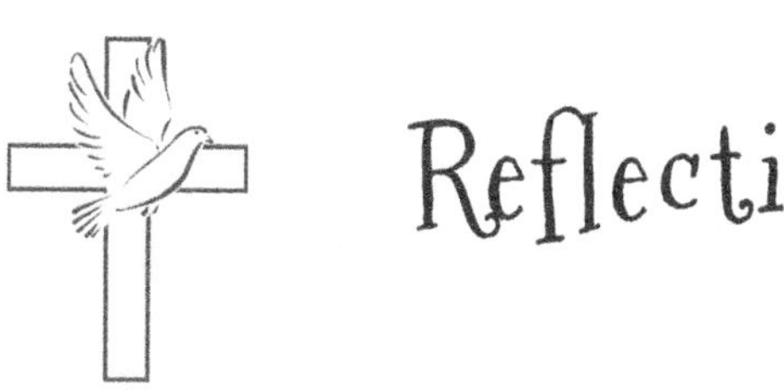

Reflection

With God, we will always have the fortitude to tackle life's obstacles. Do you believe you represent God? Why do you think that?

PART 2

Prayers for Hope

Prayer for Comfort

*

God is our refuge and strength, a very present help in trouble. Therefore will not we fear, though the earth be removed, and though the mountains be carried into the midst of the sea. Though the waters thereof roar and be troubled, though the mountains shake with the swelling thereof.

Psalms 46:1-3

Prayer

Sacred Father in Heaven, My eyes fill with tears, and I toss and turn all night because of my loneliness and despair. Be my safe haven, replacing my sadness with calm and my source of strength when I feel feeble and unable to go on. When my emotions drag me down, and I feel hopeless, help me confidently believe you are in charge. Bring me solace and healing, and help me to rest easy. In the name of Jesus, amen.

*

Reflection

We should seek God's assistance when confronted with difficulties. Who always assists you in times of need? How do you assist those with problems?

Prayer for Help

These things I have spoken unto you, that in me ye might have peace. In the world ye shall have tribulation: but be of good cheer; I have overcome the world.

John 16:33

Prayer

Creator God, Things in my life seem confusing right now. I'm responsible for part of it, other people have a hand in it, and some of it simply appears to have happened to me. On occasion, I feel anger; on others, I feel humiliation. Put decent, kind individuals in my way, please. Thank you, God, for allowing me to make good decisions. Hear my heartfelt plea for help. In the name of Jesus, amen.

Reflection

God is always there to assist us; we just need to ask. Who do you believe needs assistance the most right now? What will you do to help this person?

Prayer for Loss

And God shall wipe away all tears from their eyes; and there shall be no more death, neither shall there be any more pain: for the former things are passed away.

Revelation 21:4

Prayer

Heavenly Father, I have suffered the loss of a loved one. A sense of sorrow has grown like a constant companion. I want you to facilitate my grieving process so that the ache of loss might be soothed and eventually healed. I hope to one day reminisce about these times without feeling such intense sadness. To smile gently and lovingly at the memory of my beloved. God, I pray that you will help me heal. Amen.

❃

Reflection

Losing a loved one is difficult, but God can provide the solace we need. Have you ever lost a loved one? How did you overcome your loss?

Prayer for Guidance

✻

Thy word is a lamp unto my feet and a light unto my path.

Psalms 119:105

Prayer

Holy God, I don't know where to turn, but your promise will lead me home. I pray that my heart, like a garden whose roots are deep in your love, may flourish due to your care. Please let me put my faith in you and the choices you'll help me make in the future. Instead of depending on my limited knowledge, please hold me close. Please direct me in a way that I can understand. Kindly point me in the right direction, please. Persuade me that following in your footsteps is always the smartest choice. In the name of Jesus, amen.

Reflection

God constantly leads us along the correct road in life. What do you want to accomplish in life? How would you know your route will bring you to your life goals?

Prayer for the Worried

Be careful for nothing; but in everything by prayer and supplication with thanksgiving let your requests be made known unto God.

Philippians 4:6

Prayer

When my heart is heavy and full of sorrow, God brings me peace. So much of my time is consumed with contemplation, preparation, and fretting about my future. In the midst of chaos, help me to put my faith in you. Please assist me in taking the right actions and making the right life choices. I need your assistance finding some peace. Let me rest easy knowing you care for me and are always here. Holy Spirit, lead my thoughts and emotions toward peace in Christ. Amen.

✻

Reflection

If we seek tranquility, we must believe in and obey God. What concerns do you have today? How can you prevent yourself from worrying excessively?

Prayer in Uncertain Times

I have set the Lord always before me: because he is at my right hand, I shall not be moved.

Psalms 16:8

Prayer

When my heart is heavy and full of sorrow, God brings me peace. So much of my time is consumed with contemplation, preparation, and fretting about my future. In the midst of chaos, help me to put my faith in you. Please assist me in taking the right actions and making the right life choices. I need your assistance finding some peace. Let me rest easy knowing you care for me and are always here. Holy Spirit, lead my thoughts and emotions toward peace in Christ. Amen.

✱

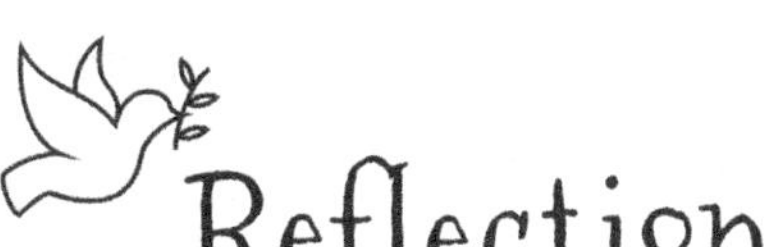

Reflection

If we seek tranquility, we must believe in and obey God. What concerns do you have today? How can you prevent yourself from worrying excessively?

We are Tired and Weary

*

Therefore is my spirit overwhelmed within me; my heart within me is desolate. I remember the days of old; I meditate on all thy works; I muse on the work of thy hands. I stretch forth my hands unto thee: my soul thirsteth after thee, as a thirsty land.

Psalms 143:4-6

Prayer

Eternal and Undying Father, All the time, all the minute, I need You. Have mercy on me and shower me with Your unending affection. Please watch over me as I enter today's cold, unforgiving world. I pray that today, Oh Loving Lord, You will bless me with a sense of Your holy, calming presence while I am weary and weak and my soul is filled with despair. Don't make me give up amid this weariness. In the name of Jesus Christ, amen.

Reflection

Our loads grow lighter when we relax and allow God to bear them on our behalf. What is making you weary at the moment? What is your understanding of rest?

I Surrender All

Now the God of hope fills you with all joy and peace in believing, that ye may abound in hope, through the power of the Holy Ghost

Romans 15:13.

Prayer

Lord, I give everything to You. Lord, I hope I comprehend the part you assigned me to play on this path. Help me understand the reason behind Your plan. Give me the courage, hope, and strength to take the next step toward my goal. Help me, Lord, to walk in the way You have ordained for me while I seek Your face. Help my tired soul relax into Your everlasting calm. Please grant me the indescribable pleasure of dancing in the rain! To God be the glory forever and ever, amen.

Reflection

God has a plan for each person, and we should always endeavor to follow it. What do you believe is God's will for you? How does your family assist you in accomplishing God's will for your life?

PART 3

Prayers for Thanksgiing

Prayer of Thanks for God's Help

*

I will praise thee, O Lord, with my whole heart; I will show forth all thy marvelous works.

Psalms 9:1

Prayer

Today, Lord, I offer you my undivided gratitude. Enable me to share the news of your great works with others. You've been helpful and kind, and I appreciate everything you've done. As I go about my day, may I never forget the countless ways you have blessed me, and may I always be quick to give thanks to you. Amen.

*

Reflection

We should constantly share God's good news with people. How has God assisted you with today's tasks? How would you introduce people to God?

Prayer of Thanks for the Congregation

*

I will give thee thanks in the great congregation: I will praise thee among many people.

- Psalms 35:18

Prayer

Thank you, Lord, that we may worship you here in this magnificent congregation. I honor your name in the presence of my loved ones, friends, and fellow churchgoers. When I praise and offer thanks to you, I announce to people around me that you are good and in charge of my life. Praise God, for today, I can put my faith in you. Amen.

*

Reflection

The essential substance of the church of Christ consists of those who worship him as a unified body. How often do you attend church? What encourages you to attend church routinely?

Prayer of Thanks for Triumph

*

But I am poor and sorrowful: let thy salvation, O God, set me up on high. I will praise the name of God with a song and will magnify him with thanksgiving.

Psalms 69:29-30

Prayer

Even when I suffer, may I never forget the triumph of my redemption in you. You will always pull me through, no matter how bad things become. Please help me express my gratitude by praising you in song. Simply put, I am aware of your excellence and know I can always rely on you. Amen.

*

Reflection

God will always enable us to overcome every difficulty. How do you manage your problems? How do you overcome your troubles?

Prayer of Thanks for God's Salvation

*

O come, let us sing unto the Lord: let us make a joyful noise to the rock of our salvation. Let us come before his pres ence with thanksgiving and make a joyful noise unto him with psalms.

Psalms 95:1-2

Prayer

Lord, thank you because you are my salvation's solid foundation. Even when everything else around me seems to crumble, I know you are the rock I may safely stand on because of your unwavering love, serenity, and grace. Your steadfastness has been a source of comfort to me, and I am grateful for the psalms of gratitude that help me to remember this. Amen.

*

Reflection

God alone is our savior. Who is your favorite hero? Why do you like him the most?

Prayer of Thanks for God's Unfailing Love

*

Make a joyful noise unto the Lord, all ye lands. Serve the Lord with gladness: come before his presence with singing. Know ye that the Lord he is God: it is he that hath made us, and not we ourselves; we are his people and the sheep of his pasture.

Psalms 100:1-3

Prayer

Praise the Lord that I can worship you with music. Every nation will give a joyful scream in your honor. I thank you that I am made in your likeness. Lord, you are my Good Shepherd; you will guide and direct my steps from this day forward. Because of your unfailing love and loyalty, my family and I will be blessed for many years. Amen.

*

Reflection

God loves us unconditionally. How much do you adore God? How do you express your love for him?

Prayer of Thanks for God's Understanding

O Lord, thou hast searched me, and know me. Thou knowest my downsitting and mine uprising, thou understandest my thought afar off.

Psalms 139:1-2

Prayer

I thank you, Father, for understanding me better than I understand myself. That you have a complete and thorough understanding of and love for me is beyond words. Despite our physical distance, you are always in my mind. I bow down to your superior wisdom, as it is beyond me to comprehend everything all at once. Amen.

*

Reflection

God alone understands us and is the only one who genuinely knows us. What type of person do you consider yourself to be? What kind of person do people perceive you to be?

Prayer of Thanks for God's Strength

And said, I beseech thee, O Lord God of heaven, the great and terrible God, that keepeth covenant and mercy for them that love him and observe his commandments.

Nehemiah 1:5

Prayer

God, I'm glad you're not a weak 'god' that can't handle the scale of things. You, Lord, are the Almighty God. Because you created the universe, you are responsible for keeping it going strong. Every aspect of my life is possible because of you, and I am eternally grateful. When it comes to the people who love you, you never break your word. Today, I need your help putting my faith in your words. In the name of Jesus, I ask this, amen.

*

Reflection

God is larger than our difficulties and stronger than our adversaries. What does it mean to you to be strong? Where do you get the strength to confront all your difficulties?

Prayer of Thanks for God's Grace

Being confident of this very thing, that he which hath begun a good work in you will perform it until the day of Jesus Christ.

Philippians 1:6

Prayer

God, you have promised to be with me even in the midst of my despair. I appreciate your faith in me and your refusal to abandon the excellent work you began in me. Whenever I feel like I have nowhere else to turn, I am shown grace and compassion. Grace is so freely given in you, Jesus, and I am grateful that it is impossible for me to lose or earn it back. Amen.

*

Reflection

God will still love and forgive us despite our transgressions. What do you do when someone hurts you? Do you think everyone deserves to be forgiven, and if so, why?

PART 4

Prayers for Family and Friends

A Thanksgiving Prayer For Family And Friends

*

And the Lord turned the captivity of Job when he prayed for his friends: also the Lord gave Job twice as much as he had before.

Job 42:10

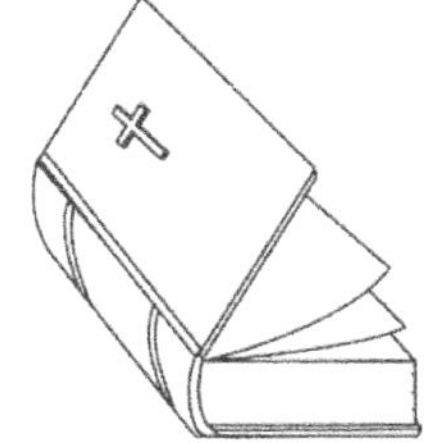

Prayer

Lord, I appreciate You so much for the wonderful friends and family You've put in my path. They are always there to help me when I'm feeling down. It is through them that You reveal Your divine presence to me. Because of the people who love me, I know You are always around. I pray for my loved ones to You with a heart filled with thankfulness. I am grateful that You have enlightened me that kindness and compassion are everywhere, particularly in the individuals we encounter. Amen.

*

Reflection

Our family and friends are blessings from God. How do you express your affection for your family? How do you decide on somebody to befriend?

A Short Prayer For Family

*

We love him because he first loved us.

J1 John 4:19

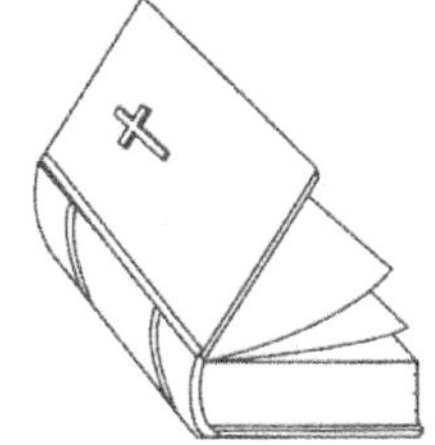

Prayer

The Highest God, I thank You and honor Your holy name. My family and I are grateful for another day to revel in the many gifts You have given us. Please hear my humble plea for Your continued protection of my family and friends. If they are happy now, please don't let that joy leave Your protective arms. You are the glue that holds us together, and as long as our hearts are focused on You, our love for one another will never falter. Amen.

*

Reflection

God's love for us is manifested in our family. How often do you tell your family that you love them? What blessing would you wish for your family?

Prayer For Family Protection

But let all those that put their trust in thee rejoice: let them ever shout for joy, because thou defendest them: let them also that love thy name be joyful in thee.

Psalms 5:11

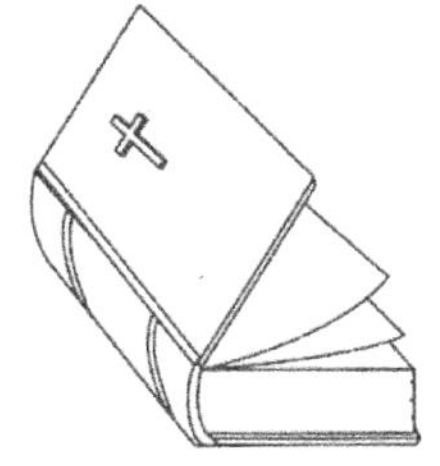

Prayer

Please know how grateful I am that You have always kept my loved ones from danger, Dear God. Even though we are physically apart, we are still a unified spiritual family. Our shared belief in God brings us together no matter how close or far apart we are. My loved ones' continued security is something I pray for every day. No matter where we are, we are always under Your watchful eye. The safety of our family unit depends on our shared commitment to following Your lead. This I ask of you in the name of Jesus Christ, amen.

*

Reflection

God will always safeguard our family as he protects us. How does your family preserve a close connection with God? How frequently does your family pray?

Prayer For Healing For A Family Member

*

To everything, there is a season, and a time to every purpose under heaven: A time to be born, and a time to die; a time to plant, and a time to pluck up that which is planted.

Ecclesiastes 3:1-2

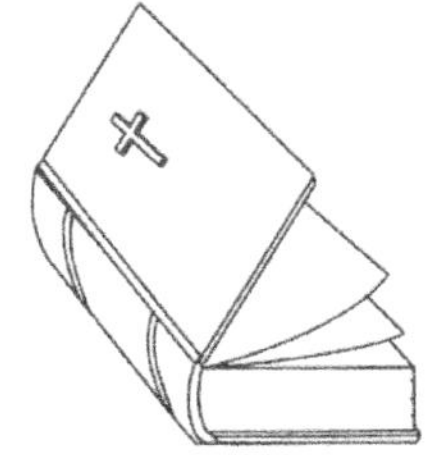

Prayer

Blessed and Holy Father, I come to You because someone in my family is going through a very painful time. They need You, our greatest strength, now more than ever. Please give them the strength to keep going despite the overwhelming difficulty of their situation. I hope that the ache in their chest may lessen to a faint throb that Your kind love can soothe. Praise be to the Lord! Amen.

*

Reflection

God is our great healer, and we can always ask him to heal our loved ones. Who in your family is currently in need of healing? How do you believe you can aid in his healing?

Morning Prayer For My Family

*

Let love be without dissimulation. Abhor that which is evil; cleave to that which is good.

Romans 12:9

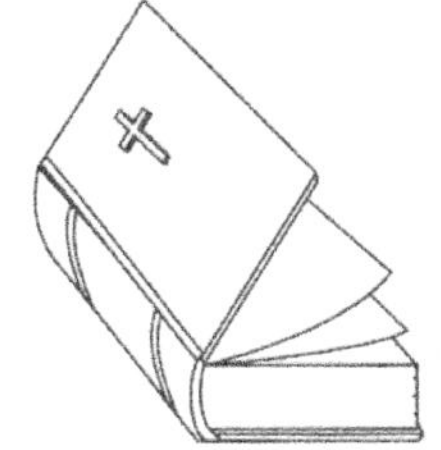

Prayer

God in the heavens, I praise You for another day so that I may do Your will. At the dawn of a new day, I pray to You. I ask You, Lord, to please help my loved ones keep You at the forefront of each day. Give them Your fortitude to face whatever the day brings with grace and serenity. We ask that You anoint them with Your Holy Spirit so that they may always remember that, with You at their side, everything is possible, no matter how challenging the day ahead may appear. Amen.

*

Reflection

Always pray for God's direction and protection before beginning each day. How do you start your day? How does your family begin each day?

Prayer For Family Peace

✻

If it be possible, as much as lieth in you, live peaceably with all men.

Romans 12:18

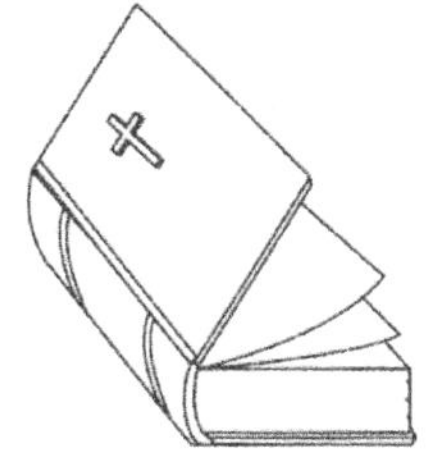

Prayer

Our hearts are divided as we approach You, the most wonderful Lord. Right now, things are difficult for our family. Lord, have mercy on us for falling into the evil of hostility. There is love between us; thus, we are not trying to harm one another. To You, we pray for the strength to work together to mend the rifts in our family. Please let us be able to forgive the hurt we've caused one other. We beg You to help us put this disagreement behind us so we may serve You as one unified family. Amen.

*

Reflection

Family conflicts are normal, but we should always seek to resolve them as quickly as possible. How do you resolve conflicts within your family? What do you do when a family member hurts you?

Prayer For Guidance And Wisdom For My Parents

*

I have taught thee in the way of wisdom; I have led thee in the right paths.

Proverbs 4:11

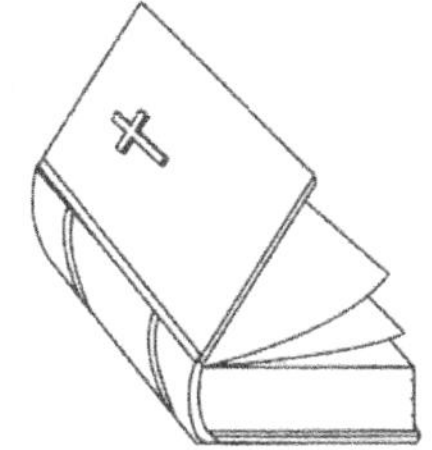

Prayer

God the Father, Please don't stop protecting my mom and dad from harm because they mean the world to me. They introduced me to You and instructed me to become your devoted disciple. Please bestow Your mercy on them; no matter our age, we gain knowledge from You daily. I pray that You will give my parents the insight they need and that they will never forget that You are always with them, no matter what they face. This I ask in the name of Jesus Christ, our Lord, amen.

*

Reflection

Our parents are our first and foremost teachers and guardians. What are the characteristics of your parents? How did they first introduce you to God?

Daily Prayer For Friends

*

Wherefore comfort yourselves together, and edify one another, even as also ye do.

1 Thessalonians 5:11

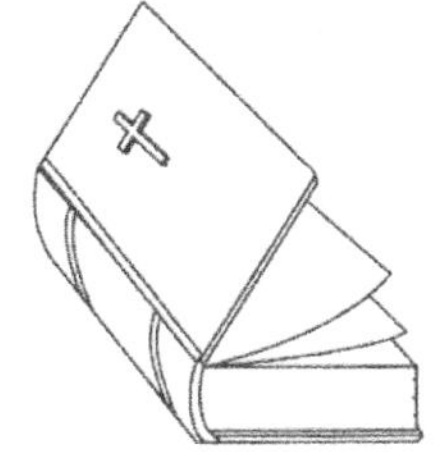

Prayer

My God, I am grateful to You for the friends You have given me. Knowing that I can always rely on them brings immeasurable happiness and affection into my days. Even though I don't always tell them, I hope they know in their hearts how much they mean to me. Lord, please watch my friends as they go about their everyday lives. I know our relationship would not be what it is now without You. I hope You continue to bless our relationship with Your presence because it would not be what it is today without You. Amen.

*

Reflection

True friends will always be there for you regardless of the circumstances. Who is your best friend? Why do you see him as your closest friend?

PART 5

Prayers for Encouragement

I will wait upon the Lord

But they that wait upon the Lord shall renew their strength; they shall mount up with wings as eagles; they shall run, and not be weary; and they shall walk, and not faint.

Isaiah 40:31

Prayer

Father in Heaven, when we are at a loss for what to do next, you always come through, and for that, I am eternally grateful. We are grateful for the lessons you've given us about patience and how to serve You better as we wait. Having confidence in Your abilities and knowing what to anticipate from You as a result of receiving Your favor brings tremendous satisfaction. Because only You, Father, know the finest and most appropriate course of action, so we will wait for You. In the name of Jesus Christ, we ask this, amen.

*

Reflection

God will enlighten our hearts and minds when we are puzzled by our circumstances. What one question do you want to ask God at this time? What do you do if God does not answer your prayers?

Prayer To Overcome Fear And Worry

Know therefore that the Lord thy God, he is God, the faithful God, which keepeth covenant and mercy with them that love him and keep his commandments to a thousand generations.

Deuteronomy 7:9

Prayer

God, I know I fail you sometimes. I fight to cling to Your assurances, yet other forces keep trying to dominate me. For me, it's important that negative emotions like worry, anxiety and fear never get in the way of realizing my goals. Give me the strength to be moved by Jesus's example. I beg You, Lord, to change my heart and refresh my thinking in the places where I fall short. Lord, please do miracles in my life so I may be encouraged. I need the motivation to accomplish what You have planned for me. Amen.

*

Reflection

It is natural to fail sometimes, but this should drive us to fight even more. What is your biggest fear? What effect does this fear have on your connection with God?

Prayer For Strength And Inspiration Throughout The Day

*

The steps of a good man are ordered by the Lord: and he delighteth in his way. Though he falls, he shall not be utterly cast down: for the Lord upholdeth him with his hand..

Psalms 37:23-241

Prayer

Divine Father, please hear my prayer. I feel exhausted, spent, weak, and weary. Because of you, Nonetheless, I shall make it through this since You are my fortitude whenever I am frightened or alone. You provide me with a stable foundation to rely on. You are a source of renewed energy whenever I seek you out. Remove any barriers that stand in my path. Since one's words have the power of life and death, I choose to speak only words of good fortune and hope into my existence. Amen.

*

Reflection

We should begin each day with prayer. What do your morning prayers consist of? What effect does morning devotion have on you?

Prayer For God's Timing

For the vision is yet for an appointed time, but at the end, it shall speak, and not lie: though it tarries, wait for it; because it will surely come, it will not tarry.

Habakkuk 2:3

Prayer

Your seat of grace is where mercy is found, and it is there that I come to adore You, Lord. I am forever grateful to You, heavenly Father, for always hearing and responding to my prayers. Have mercy on me, God, and grant me the patience to wait for your perfect time. God, I know that things won't always go the way I plan or anticipate. However, you always find a way to make things better for me. I have faith in Your time and know that it is always right. Amen.

*

Reflection

Everything we pray for will be granted in God's perfect timing. How valuable is time to you? How many hours per week do you devote to God?

Give Me Patience

*

But, beloved, be not ignorant of this one thing, that one day is with the Lord as a thousand years, and a thousand years as one day. The Lord is not slack concerning his promise, as some men count slackness, but is longsuffering to us-ward, not willing that any should perish, but that all should come to repentance.

2 Peter 3:8-9

Prayer

Lord, I submit my will and my life to you. Please, Heavenly Father, may Your unending love continue to flood my soul as long as I remain upright. I pray that God's tranquility will accompany me throughout my daily life. Please grant me the patience to wait for you to sort everything out. Lord, strengthen my confidence in your promises and your time. I trust in the truths that you have said. Amen.

*

Reflection

We should be patient while we await God's answers since he works in mysterious ways. Do you believe the promises God has made to you? Why do you hold this belief?

Waiting On The Manifestation

✻

And let us not be weary in well doing: for in due season we shall reap if we faint not. .

Galatians 6:91

Prayer

The Most High God, You instruct us to be patient and steadfast while we wait to fulfill our supplications. We thank you for the confidence you've given us to wait for you to answer our supplications and prayers at the right moment. You have impeccable timeliness and always address our most pressing issues. Many thanks to God the Father for the incomparable Jesus Christ. In the name of God, the most High, amen.

*

Reflection

God responds to our requests in ways we least anticipate. What prayer has God lately answered for you? How did God respond to your prayer?

Prayer When Let Down

Uphold me according unto thy word, that I may live: and let me not be ashamed of my hope.

Psalms 119:116

Prayer

Lord, you know how difficult it is for us to deal with the disappointments of life and the disappointments of others. Make it clear to us that You are the reliable, eternal Father. As a God, you never leave us or abandon us. Let us know that even when we are disappointed, it is part of Your plan to teach us something and make us better people overall. Amen.

*

Reflection

There is always something to be learned from failure or disappointment. Have you ever let other people down? Why did they feel let down by you?

Replacing All That's Lost

*

But as for you, ye thought evil against me; but God meant it unto good, to bring to pass, as it is this day, to save much people alive..

Genesis 50:20

Prayer

Peaceful times in your presence are available at any hour, Lord. Keep us close as we find refuge in You. Help us to remain focused and collected as we navigate the turbulent currents. Show us how to wait patiently while You bring forth better alternatives. While the night may bring grief, the dawn always brings a new chance for happiness. When setbacks arise, we pledge in the name of Jesus to be calm and patient, knowing that the Lord will provide our needs in proportion to the wealth of His glory. Amen.

*

Reflection

God will always replace what we lose with something greater. What is the one thing you would not want to lose? Why do you not want this to be lost?

PART 6

Prayers for Healing

Healing Of Bodily Diseases

*

The centurion answered and said, Lord, I am not worthy that thou shouldest come under roof: but speak the word only, and my servant shall be healed.

Matthew 8:8

Prayer

It was You, Lord Jesus Christ, who took on yourself our pain and anguish. I pray that the healing power of Your holy name may rest upon my body and restore health where it is lacking. Just as You cleansed the lepers, restore the health of those who have been afflicted by bodily ailments, please remove whatever spiritual leprosy I may have as I fall at Your feet and ask forgiveness for disobeying the Father by going against His word and His desire. No sickness cannot be cured by the power of the Name of Jesus. Amen.

*

Reflection

God is our great healer and can cure us of any ailment. What do you do if you're ill? How do you care for your own health?

Command and Declare Healing

*

The Lord is my strength and song, and he has become my salvation: he is my God, and I will prepare him a habitation; my father's God, and I will exalt him.

Exodus 15:2

Prayer

Using the glorious and holy name of Jesus Christ, my Lord, and Savior, I pray to you, O God. I give thanks to You for the daily revelations of Your kindness. To You, O Lord, be the glory. Please accept my gratitude for all the ways in which You have blessed me so far. As I continue to praise You, O God, I pledge always to invoke a blessing upon Your name. I will always speak highly of you. In You, I find safety and strength, and it is in You that I find my very existence. Amen.

✻

Reflection

God constantly cures the sick; thus, he is worthy of all praise and gratitude. What does spiritual healing entail? What has God lately healed you from?

I Declare Healing

But he was wounded for our transgressions, he was bruised for our iniquities: the chastisement of our peace was upon him, and with his stripes, we are healed.

Isaiah 53:5

Prayer

Holy God, my Healer, I give praise to Jesus Christ, whose name is without equal. I hereby decree that every yoke placed upon me is shattered. Anything that sets itself up in opposition to the truth about God is brought crashing down and thrown into the ocean. Through the combined efforts of the Father, the Son, and the Holy Spirit, any obstacle may be overcome. Amen.

Reflection

Jesus died on the cross in order to heal the world. How did the death of Jesus heal the world? How can we honor the sacrifice Jesus made for us?

A Prayer Against Disease

*

Beloved, I wish above all things that thou mayest prosper and be in health, even as thy soul prospereth.

3 John 1:2

Lord, have the power to cure any illness and that those who put their faith in you will not perish but have eternal life. In order to save us from our sins and give us access to heaven, you sacrificed your life by dying on the cross and rising from the dead. I have faith that you are here with us now and will use your most holy power to rid the world of all its ills. Please, Lord, have your way. In the name of Jesus, I decree full and utter healing. With thanksgiving and adoration, we honor and celebrate your name. Amen.

*

Throughout his time on earth, Jesus performed miraculous healings. Which of the biblical accounts of Jesus curing the sick is your favorite? Why does this appeal to you the most?

Prayer for Healing From Abuse

*

The Lord is not slack concerning his promise, as some men count slackness; but is longsuffering to us-ward, not willing that any should perish, but that all should come to repentance.

2 Peter 3:9

Prayer

In your presence, Almighty Lord, I offer you my highest worship. To You, I devote all my love and devotion. Precious Savior, Any chronic ailment that has been plaguing me, I renounce in the name of Jesus. Lord, save me from anyone who would hurt me in any way, whether physically, mentally, or emotionally. Show me the way to a peaceful and loving relationship with others for the glory of God the Father and the salvation of Jesus Christ, Amen.

*

Reflection

Only God can cure us of whatever physical, mental, or emotional abuse we may have suffered. What effect does abuse have on our spiritual health? How can we prevent someone from emotionally abusing us?

Praying for the Sick

And the Lord shall guide thee continually, and satisfy thy soul in drought, and make fat thy bones: and thou shalt be like a watered garden, and like a spring of water, whose waters fail not.

Isaiah 58:11

Prayer

Holy Father, I beg you, please extend your hand right now. Put Your healing hands on each one of us. The rivers of my life are churning with anxiety; please pour Your serenity onto them. You can never forget the pleadings of the humble, Lord; that's why you must keep a firm grasp on our hand. With Your loving hand guiding us firmly but tenderly, grant us Your perfect calm so we may battle our way back to health and wealth. please cover us with Your tremendous healing and Your real constancy. In the mighty name of Jesus Christ, Your only begotten Son, we humbly beg of You. Amen.

Reflection

Prayer for our ailing loved ones is an excellent technique to aid in their recovery from their disease. How do you alleviate someone's pain? What do you do when a family member is sick?

Heal the Broken Spirit

✻

No weapon that is formed against thee shall prosper; and every tongue that shall rise against thee in judgment thou shalt condemn. This is the heritage of the servants of the Lord, and their righteousness is of me, saith the Lord.

Isaiah 54:17

Prayer

Even though our hearts are heavy and shattered, we come to you, O Great and Gracious God, to express our gratitude for your amazing grace. Thank you for being kind and loving despite our many faults. We are grateful that you sent your Son, Jesus Christ, to die on the cross for our sins and restore us to fellowship with yourself. We praise you for the comfort of your peace beyond all comprehension and the kindness of your unending mercy. Amen.

*

Reflection

God's healing is not just physical but spiritual as well. Why do our spirits become broken? What happens when we lose our spirit?

Hear The Cries Of The Broken

*

And the peace of God, which passeth all understanding, shall keep your hearts and minds through Christ Jesus.

Philippians 4:7

Prayer

Father in Heaven, we pray to you. Jesus, please listen to our prayers. You have promised to be there whenever two or more people pray to you in Jesus' name. Since you're here with us, we will go ahead and announce that every broken spirit is now whole and well. Father God, I praise you for restoring hope and strength to the discouraged and the weak. Amen.

*

Reflection

Our God can accomplish anything for us; therefore, we should assert that we will prevail in any struggle. Do you believe yourself to be healed of all your brokenness? Why do you say so?

Encouragement to Continue Praying

"Be careful for nothing, but in everything by prayer and supplication with thanksgiving let your requests be made known unto God."

- Philippians 4:6

Praying, the simplest Christian practice elicits a wide range of reactions and interpretations among Christians. Some people keep praying because they feel God hears them, while others have given up or stopped praying as often because they believe God isn't paying attention. But His ears are perked up, and He is actively listening.

Just as your earthly parents would want to hear from and converse with you, so would your Heavenly Father. As you call out to God, He will hear you. Then He answers your prayers in the shape of ideas, spiritual sensations, scripture, or other people's behavior. According to the Bible, God is love (1 John 4:8). If you pray to God daily and ask for direction, you will begin to experience His unconditional love. One of the best ways to figure out what you were here to do was to talk to God about it. If you seek Him, God will reveal your purpose for being here and the steps you need to take to spend eternity in His presence.

Praying alone to God may help you sort through life's toughest choices. God is attentive to our prayers and often responds with the precise wisdom we need. Prayer itself may provide calm, even if God doesn't respond immediately or as we'd want. If you want to avoid temptation, Jesus told His followers, "Watch and pray that you enter not into temptation" (Matthew 26:41). Sinful urges may be resisted by prayer. Try asking God to guide your decisions and prevent you from making any blunders. This will fortify you to act morally.

Praying isn't always about telling God what you want Him to do. Rather, it's about growing in the knowledge of God and His ways and ultimately coming into harmony with His will. Praying "doesn't alter God," as C. S. Lewis is commonly quoted as saying. "It makes me change." When it came to praying, Jesus was the epitome of perfection. You may become more like Him by imitating His prayer life and strengthening your connection to God the Father.

Prayer is a means to connect with God, our loving Heavenly Father. When we pray to him, he always hears us. Praying regularly may benefit your life and the lives of others you pray for. It can help you discover more about God's will for your life, provide you with more inner peace, and do much more besides.

Quiz Questions

Complete the Sentence Questions

1. Sing unto the Lord with __________; sing praise upon the harp unto our God.

    a. praise

    b. thanksgiving

    c. joy

2. Let the words of my mouth, and the meditation of my heart, be acceptable in thy sight, O Lord, my strength, and my __________.

    a. redeemer

    b. savior

    c. life

3. For God hath not given us the spirit of __________; but of power, and of love, and of a sound mind.

    a. love

    b. Jesus

    c. fear

4. And God shall wipe away all tears from their eyes, and there shall be no more death, nor shall there be any more __________: for the former things are passed away.

a. pain

b. suffering

c. enemies

5. I have set the Lord always before me: because he is at my __________, I shall not be moved.

a. side

b. heart

c. right hand

6. I will praise thee, O Lord, with my whole heart; I will show forth all thy __________ works.

a. beautiful

b. wonderful

c. marvelous

7. O Lord, thou hast __________ me, and know me. Thou knowest my downsitting and mine uprising, thou understandest my thought afar off.

a. pursued

b. searched

c. abandoned

8. We love him because he first __________ us.

a. loved

b. created

c. gifted

Quiz Answer:

1. b. thanksgiving
2. a. redeemer
3. c. fear
4. a. pain
5. c. right hand
6. c. marvelous
7. b. searched
8. a. loved
9. a. cleave
10. b. reap
11. c. hope
12. a. evil

Don't Forget Your Free Bonus Downloads!

As our way of saying thank you, we've included in every purchase bonus gift downloads. If you've enjoyed reading this book, please consider leaving a review.

Or Scan Your Phone to open QR code

About Us

FaithLabs is a faith-based publisher dedicated to producing books that inspire and uplift readers.

With a focus on Christian values and principles, FaithLab's team of experienced editors work closely with authors to bring their messages of hope and faith to life. From devotional books to inspirational memoirs, FaithLabs offers a range of titles to deepen readers' spiritual journeys.

Thanks for reading,

FAITH LABS

Made in the USA
Monee, IL
13 January 2025